Pop Academy of Music Storybook Collection

Spaces of the Treble Clef

Traditional mnemonics systems teach you to learn in sequence - Every, Good, Boy, Does, Fine. However, what happens when you want to identify the notes out of sequence, quickly. Think quickly, you have one second, what is the third space of the Treble Clef? The answer can be hard for some and impossible for others, even if you know the Mnemonic method F-A-C-E, which is generally taught to remember the spaces.

The key to retaining the information out of sequence is to add and create more neuro-associations. Research has proven that neuro-connections have a lasting effect on a child's ability to recognize symbols. This is why we teach the alphabet in connection with an object. A is for Apple. Most adults, even years later, can recognize the neuro-connection that they made in kindergarten. You later associated letters with words, and words with songs, stories, and lessons.

This is the approach, the Sozo Music Teaching System takes, and we teach the musical alphabet in association with a fun-loving character that can be found on both our piano stickers and our sheet music. Then we associate that musical alphabet with words, songs, stories, poems, and lessons.

The Sozo Music Teaching System is a 5-part system that includes the Piano book, the Pop Academy of Music Storybook Collection, Read and Play CD, Practice Midi Files, and our special Sozo piano stickers. To learn more please visit us at Popacademyofmusic.com

Pop Academy of Music

Copyright © 2013 T.S. Cherry

All rights reserved.

ISBN-10:0-9887710-8-X

ISBN-13:978-0-9887710-8-6

LCCN Imprint Name: Pop Academy of Music

Contents

Chapter 1
In Search of a Human Child..1

Chapter 2
Spaces of the Treble Clef..14

Chapter 3
The Dog Who Could See in Color...20

Chapter 4
Quest of the Oracle..23

Chapter 5
No'Moda..33

Chapter 6
Le' Cat and the Twelve Spies...35

Chapter 7
Michael the Pooka...43

Chapter 8
Tales of the Merfish..49

Glossary and Terms..57

Chapter One
In Search of a Human Child

Far away in the magical Land of Sozo, Elvis the King and his brother Middleton Cat watched the keynotes from the window of the Great Sozo Palace. Elvis, being the King of the Treble Clef Kingdom, was fond of his visits with his brother.

You see, Middleton Cat often traveled between the Treble Clef Kingdom and the Bass Clef Kingdom in hopes of uniting the two kingdoms, but this was different. This day they conceived a plan in order to change the fate of their land. They realized a human child was needed to overcome the evil self-appointed guardian, No'meda, who divided the kingdoms through the unseen world.

Once the crowds of Keynotes had gone on their way, the King and his brother would return to the massive table where they would continue their work to bring the two Kingdoms together.

Today marked a new revelation in the progress of their plans. With the slyness of a cat, Middleton had created a plan to get the Land of Sozo into the human world, thereby uniting the kingdoms.

"We will use a method as old as time itself. We will use a book." Middleton told his brother. "Pinned in an unforeseen path to us, the child will experience the captivating world of both love and music."

The King looked at his brother as he considered this book idea. Books containing wisdom had withstood time.

"This book idea has promise," the King said. "What should we call it?"

Middleton gave his brother a huge grin and answered, "*The Ape in the Mirror*."

"You don't mean *The Chromatic Apes*?" The King asked.

"I do, indeed!" Middleton replied.

Both brothers were delighted, their endless days and nights of searching for an answer to unite the two kingdoms may finally be over.

"What a brilliant idea," the King said.

"It came from something I read this week in our library of wisdom." Middleton added,

> *"The seed of the promise, birthed not from you,*
> *hinges on another world that can make one of two."*

"Yes, I remember the legend! The Son of Eve will destroy evil and restore the kingdoms."

The King then understood his brother's choice of the Chromatic Apes; those attracted to the book would share their characteristics of being passionate, protective, fun loving, loyal, and brave.

The King threw his head back and smiled as he thought about the great joy the Chromatic Apes bought to their land.

"This book, *The Ape in the Mirror*, will take the human child through the life of one very special Chromatic Ape, Levi the Great!" Middleton explained. "Once the child can sees himself as Levi, his world will forever be changed. With each page, the child's imagination will take over, until the human child becomes the second space of the Treble Clef Staff."

"This will work!" exclaimed the King.

"Yes, I'm sure of it! The child will look into their mirror and be transported to our Park of True Identity." Middleton agreed.

Then the brothers called on one of the wisest goats in their providence, Billy, to create the book. He was by trade, an Egend of potions, a friend of the trees, connected to the land itself. They had unlocked the secrets of the land and the trees to create many books before this. The land and the trees knew everything, and nothing was known outside of them.

Billy pinned the book with the ink of fairy fish wishes. The paper was made from gold leaves, the emblem was carved from branches taken from the Tree of Sozo, dipped in the sea of purpose, and then forged in the dragon's breath of both fire and ice. The emblem that emerged was unlike anything any keynote had ever seen.

This special book, T*he Ape in the Mirror*, would be in every library where human children were sure to be found.

Once the books were in the libraries, it wasn't long before students began reading them. Even still, no human child yet saw himself as Levi the Great and been transported to the Land of Sozo.

A year passed, and the brothers were beginning to lose hope. Perhaps, books no longer captivated children's imaginations. However, Middleton encouraged himself by remembering that they are looking for a very special human boy!

Little did Middleton know that at the very moment he was thinking those words to himself, a special human girl, who was having trouble fitting into her school, was about to fulfill his plan.

A young girl from the Pop Academy of Music, Alley, was given an assignment to mentor a group of preschoolers. Wanting to do her best, she searched her library for books.

After several hours of searching, Alley picked up her stack of twelve books and carried them home to begin reading. Once she had all of her books set out on her bed, she began thumbing through them trying to decide which one to start with.

Then, there it was, the book with the remarkable emblem on the cover.

What a strange-looking book, Alley thought to herself.

She settled into reading the book, *The Ape in the Mirror*, the tale of two kings whose destiny was intertwined thru a battle with No'Moda, an evil sorcerer from the unseen realm. King of Salem, who would lose his life in the battle, would find an unlikely Alliance in King Levi, who would seal the fates of both tribes.

The two tribes transformed themselves into apes, in order to slip into the unseen world unnoticed through a magic mirror created by Adam. The brave men managed to destroy all doorways leading out, but one. This one door would forever change the men's destiny, and lead them to an unknown land they would later call home.

Upon their return, the two tribes were united as the Chromatic Apes under one ruler, King Levi the Great. Alley would eventually read their adventures four times before finally falling asleep.

When Alley woke up the next morning, she bolted out of bed, realizing that she had fallen asleep while reading the book. She hurried about as she dressed for school, stopping to check herself in the mirror before leaving her room.

"Ah!" Alley screamed while looking into the mirror.

Instead of her own reflection, there was an ape looking back at her. Granted, it was a fashionable ape, but it was an ape just the same. In disbelief, Alley walked closer to the full-length mirror.

"An Ape!" Alley heard herself saying while laughing. She looked down at her hands and was comforted when she realized that only her reflection was that of a Chromatic Ape.

Alley was laughing at her reflection as she waved her hands in the mirror.

Soon she could no longer see her own reflection. Instead, she saw a path of trees before her. As Alley touched her bedroom mirror, she saw her hands go straight through.

Alley pulled her hand back and stared at the path before her. Suddenly she saw the most amazing creature, a beautiful goldfish with wings like a butterfly, and arms and legs like a doll. Alley was intrigued and decided to take the unknown path through the mirror.

Looking from side to side, she stepped slowly through the mirror. It wasn't long before she looked back to question her decision. She could still see her room on the other side, but somehow, it was her room that looked like the unfamiliar world from inside the mirror.

Inside the mirror, Alley stood as tall as the trees. She was still unsure of herself when she heard a soft quiet voice telling her, "Come this way." She quickly realized that the talking trees before her were made of mirrors. Her reflection shined bright in the face of the trees.

Alley continued along the path the trees suggested, until she arrived at the large old palace that overlooks a massive garden. The Palace was frosted snow blue, with glass-vaulted ceilings and white arched cast iron doors. It wasn't long before she was surrounded by a group of small animals no larger than the toy of a human child.

Middleton had seen Alley approaching the castle as he watched from the west wing of the Palace. He quickly called out to his brother, the King, and ran to welcome her.

"A big Land of Sozo, Ktoff to you," Middleton said.

Alley's mouth dropped open as she realized that the animals could speak. "I am Middleton at your service."

"My name…is Alley," she said.

Somewhat confused, Alley looked around at the animals that were still gathering around them.

Realizing that it was time to explain everything, the King told everyone of his plan.

"Well," the King began, "you were not at all what we were expecting. Is your mother Eve, the mother of all things living on earth?"

Alley nodded her head yes, but both Middleton and the King were confused; everything they had read led them to believe that Eve's promise would come through a son, but somehow the King just knew, Alley was the key, she was the promise.

The King explained how Billy had created the special books with the extraordinary emblem on the cover.

"But, where am I?" Alley asked.

Middleton went on to describe, with great detail, the kingdom she now found herself in, The Treble Clef Kingdom.

"Throughout our kingdoms, we are known as Sozosians. And those chosen to work on the music staff are known as Keynotes." Middleton explained. "We were hoping you would help us unite our kingdoms by teaching your world about the Keynotes?"

Alley nodded and accepted the mission. Then the King and his brother handed Alley another strange looking book called, *Spaces of the Treble Clef*.

"The *Spaces of the Treble Clef* is one of eight books that chronicle our world." He said. "This book tells the spaces of the music staff of Dogs, Fishes, Apes, Cats, Elephants, and Giraffes. Most of them live within the Spaces Empire of our Treble Clef Kingdom."

"This is Allace, she's our first space. She is only a teenager, but has a lot of spirit and helps out a lot around here. Allace is called a Merfish and she… I mean they came to us from a distant land called Ork. Her tribe is the smallest here, only eight, but what they lack in number they make up in heart," he said, pointing to the rest of the Merfish.

"Our second space is the Chromatic Apes—they are the teachers of life itself. You have already read about Levi the Great and his unusual destiny; to bring two fighting kingdoms together." Alley nodded and smiled as she shook the hand of Levi the Great.

"Wow," she said, "you were brave."

"No, I was desperate," Levi responded with a smile.

"And this… this is our third space, the Valentine-Revell Cats. They are all a fun-loving family of shape shifters." The King continued. "This is Le' Cat, he is the most famous shape shifter of them all. He found the path that separated the seas and brought freedom once again to all Keynotes." Le' Cat smiled and bowed to greet Alley. Alley offered him a curtsy in return.

"Our forth space… we'll let him show you himself." The King said calling for Michael.

Michael the Pooka walked up to Alley and grew 16 feet high. Suddenly Alley, felt small.

"Wow," she said.

The King continued to introduce Michael and his tribe.

"The fourth space are mystical creatures, they have a hidden love that can unlock hidden doors."

Middleton continued to explain. Michael reached his hand out to Alley. She climbed into his hand and he showed her all the kingdoms of the land. Once Alley had met everyone, they returned to the Great Sozo Palace.

Alley took the book and began to examine the cover. On the cover, there was a brass doorknocker of a snake wrapped around a staff.

"That's a medical symbol, right." Alley said.

The Keynote smiled at Alley's response then said, "Yes, humans often use this symbol for healing the sick. It means the solution is often found in the problem."

Alley opened the book to the front-page and decided to sing the inscribed poem.

The Land of Sozo,
filled with magical places
With the lines on the staff
and all of its spaces.
The elephant, giraffe,
and the goat will be there.
We'll look really closely
to see the dancing bears.
It's the land of precious music
that we all know.
We'll all read music
from the Land of Sozo.
Yes, it's the land of precious music that we all know.
And we'll all read music from the Land of Sozo.

As Alley sang the words, something magical began to happen. The wind began to blow, and the leaves began to spin around her. When she finished reading, she looked into the eye of one of the trees and realized that her reflection had become human once again.

"When you are ready to learn more about our world, just read the book I gave you, *Spaces of the Treble Clef*." Middleton said. "This book is nicknamed *The Beginning*; it's over 6,000 years old and tells the history of some of our very special Keynotes in the Land of Sozo. Let this book be your guide"

The fear arose in Alley as her mind flooded with how unqualified she was to teach music to the world. *No Pressure*, she thought.

Then realizing the wonderful gift that they had given her, Alley hugged Middleton.

"I promise," Alley told the two brothers, "I will find a way to tell everyone about the magical Land of Sozo."

The crowd began laughing and dancing with the excitement of Alley's promise. Alley was given a chance to change the world.

"Oh," Alley gasped as she looked at her watch. "I'm late for class."

"Come back soon," the Keynotes told Alley.

Middleton gave Alley the rhyme that would transport her back home again:

"I have learned something new and met some great friends.
I have taken on a mission from a distant land.
I'm always welcome to perform in their Musical show.
But return me home; its home I must go," Alley sang.

By the end of the rhyme, she was back in her room, in front of her mirror, once again looking at her own reflection. She smiled as she grabbed her books and ran out the door to school.

Alley learned about a new kingdom. Even though she was not what they had expected, there was this feeling that she was destined for something great. Alley had waited her whole life for something to happen, but when it finally did, she wasn't sure what to make of it. She wasn't suddenly miss popular, or captain of the cheerleading team.

She settled into her chair and looked at the students around her, none of which would understand her experience. Moreover, no matter how remarkable it was, no one in the room viewed her any different then they viewed her the day before.

Alley's world would never be the same. She realized she might not have been the most qualified, the best skilled, or the most likely, but she had everything she needed to change the fate of the kingdoms in her answer of yes.

This gift was given to her from a special kingdom and was in her library for a whole year. To unlock the promise, she had to see herself as Levi the Great, the character in the book. The book led her to her purpose; without it, her destiny would be different, and perhaps, so would the Land of Sozo.

Chapter Two
Spaces of the Treble Clef

When Alley came home from school, she couldn't wait to start reading the book *Spaces of the Treble Clef*. She closed her door and lay across her bed in excitement to learn more about the Land of Sozo. She hoped the book would offer her some insight into teaching the Land of Sozo at her school. She opened the book to two trees; the first tree was elegant with wooden books growing from the branches that ascended toward the sky; the other was filled with odd-looking fruit with what appeared to be the faces of various animals. Its branches fell over and looked as if it was reaching for the ground itself.

"What interesting tree's," she thought as she began reading the story.

In the beginning, light-years from Earth, the Land of Sozo, still a new world, was about to learn an important lesson. This lesson would change the fate of the Land of Sozo forever.

What lesson, you ask? It is the lesson that a truly great leader doesn't choose where he is assigned. Instead, an assignment chooses its leaders.

On this special day in the Land of Sozo, the Parkadians were flooded with animals from near and far, wanting to teach music.

Tetris, one of the Parkadian elders, called a meeting to determine how the Keynotes would be chosen from the Sozosians that lived in the land and beyond. During the meeting, an old and wise Parkadian had an idea.

"Let's cast lots to see who will become Keynotes," he said, then stood in front of the animals and gave a wonderful speech.

"On this day, we celebrate the coming together of this great land." The wise old Parkadian said, "Music is a universal language and has brought us together. To represent the lines and the spaces of our music staff, five magical keys, each forged from ice iron, a material created by a Phoenix Dragon, will be used. In the heart of the keys is a rare gem shaped into a music note."

With a wave of his hand, the sky opened up and six keys stood before him, ready to be assigned.

"The spaces of the Treble Clef Staff are fish, ape, bear, and cat. Today, we will also be assigning the space directly above the staff—a giraffe—and the space directly below the staff—a dog." The Parkadian explained.

"We will need those species of animals to volunteer," he went on to say. "Anyone interested in these positions please stamp your family crest on a gold leaf from the Tree of Sozo." He handed everyone the leaves, a quilted pin and bottle of wishful ink.

Each interested tribe pinned its crest. The wind carried the tribal crests through the air, and then flew down into a golden bucket of life.

Tetris reached into the bucket and pulled out a leaf he hoped would represent the future of Middleton space, found below the staff. He looked at the crest and began to announce the tribe, "It looks like it will be the Chow-Chow fam—"

Before he could finish, the crest flew out of his hands and through the air. Everyone followed it to the oldest tree in the land. The crest sealed itself, with fire, inside a piece of fruit from the Tree of the upright and wicked. Everyone gasped.

A Goat by the name of Ensirjus spoke with the tree. "Judgment of love has taken place." Ensirjus said, "The tree had found the Chow-Chow Family's hearts to be wicked. This judgment is found to be final, because they have no remorse."

Everyone looked shocked as they left and returned to the bucket. The crowd was noticeably shaken by what had just transpired. Then the bucket spun around and around and around and then settled.

Suddenly, another family crest flew out of the bucket and through the air. All the Sozosians ran after the crest, as it came to a stop over the Middleton Kingdom. When they looked up to the sky, Skyworks of the family crest of the elders offered a beautiful blast of colors in the darken sky.

Tetris thought about it for a moment and said, "Middleton was chosen by our wise land! And the elders—I mean, we the Parkadian—gladly accept the assignment as the middle D note."

Everyone cheered, as they welcomed the Parkadians in the space under the Treble Clef, the Middleton Kingdom. The land set precedence that day in choosing those leaders it knew already to be leaders.

Everyone cheered as Tetris asked the Keynotes chosen that day to stand in the front. "Our Middle D is the Parkadians. For the second space of the Treble Clef Staff, we have the Chromatic Apes. Our third space of the staff is the Valentine-Revells Cats. The land has chosen the Pooka tribe for the fourth space. And last but not least, our first moon from the outer spaces of our Land of Sozo is the Oracles."

"The Land had chosen every space except the first space. We welcome the day when they are chosen." Tetris announced.

The leaves of the spaces of the Treble Clef music staff ascend to the Tree of Sozo, found in the center of the garden; each leaf became a book attached to the branches of the tree. Then the Sozoians played wonderful music to celebrate the spaces of the Treble Clef. That day would be commemorated every year as the Day of the Spaces.

"Today most of the spaces of the Treble Clef have a new assignment," Tetris said, smiling at the Oracle. "Others found lasting friendships and bonds."

It was, indeed, a special day for the Sozosians and Keynotes. They learned that love is the real key that qualifies them as leaders for an assignment.

Alley closed the book and thought about how the leaders were chosen. In her own life, she never quite saw herself as a leader, and perhaps that was Alley's biggest obstacle. Realizing who she really was would be an incredible task. I was already chosen to bring music to the human world before I ever went to the library, she thought. Who ever thought destiny was that fragile.

She went to school the next morning looking for an opportunity. When a new girl sat beside her in the cafeteria. She felt it was an opportunity for friendship. Alley introduced herself and struck up a conversation. By the end of the conversation, Alley had invited the new girl, Li, over to her house. It wasn't going to change the world, she thought. But, it did change our day.

Chapter Three
The Dog Who Could See in Color

After school, Alley was pleased that she was paying attention to the details in her life. She took her bath, did her homework and sat down on the bed to read another chapter *of Spaces of the Treble Clef*. She opened the book to the third chapter, "The Dog Who Could See in Color."

It read…There was a time, when time itself moved without clocks, watches, and without calendars.

These were the days of men. Men ruled the land with little patience for those unlike themselves. In those days, dogs were not called "man's best friend." Indeed, there was once a time when dogs were a symbol of disgrace. Originally, from the human world, the Parkadians, like other dogs, were known for their horrible behavior. They simply were impossible to train, or so everyone was led to believe.

These Parkadians were wild and known as wolves. The very mention of them would strike fear in most people. People told horrible untrue stories of attacks on young children that caused these wolves to be hunted down.

One day, a Parkadian heard a man playing beautiful music in the distance. Every morning, he would listen to him play the piano for hours on end. Finally, he approached the man. Much to the Parkadian's surprise, he discovered that the man, known to many by the name David, was blind.

David, a master piano player, was unaware of whom he was speaking. However, his friends warned him. "Send him away; he is bothering us because he cannot learn like man."

"David was silent. When he finally spoke, he agreed with the other humans, "you have been given enough chances to change your way!"

"Music is for humans," the blind man said. "It is wasted on you."

The power of David's words devastated the Parkadian. As David played his music, the Parkadian began to see beautiful colored notes coming from the piano. He never left; he simply watched and listened from a distance in amazement.

Soon enough he turned and began to journey home. As he slowly trotted through the field, his head hung low, he thought about all he would be missing. Unable to accept defeat, he turned around and headed back to David.

Gently lying at David's feet, the Parkadian said, "You are a Master, all that you have said is true. I am not worthy of your mentorship. However, if you can teach me, it will change the way every man sees me. When I see the colors—"

"You see the notes I play in color?" the master interrupted.

"Why, yes, Master," the Parkadian answered.

The master sat quietly for a moment and then said, "Explain the colors to me."

As the Parkadian explained the beautiful colors, and how every seven keys on the piano was a different color, the master began to cry.

"You can see the music notes in colors," he said. Knowing that dogs can only see in black and white, this left David puzzled. "Many upright men say you are unteachable, but you can see what no other dog can see; you shall have what you ask."

On that day, the Parkadian changed history. The bond that the Parkadian and his master formed created better lives and paved the way for other breeds of wolves to become the dogs that humans now call pets.

The Parkadian, true to his gift, taught other Parkadians and shared his love of music. They were given red hearts on their coats as a symbol, so everyone that looked upon them would know what their love for music did for all dogs.

The Parkadians became the elders of the Land of Sozo and taught man a valuable lesson. They answered the question, can a zebra change his stripes. The answer is yes, if they can find the right leader. Even those who have repeated offences can change their ways. It is this belief that helped man to recognize that a truly just man falls seven times, but still finds the strength to get back up.

Alley put the book down as she quickly realized that she was the Parkadian dog. She had gone to school several times and not been able to tell anyone about the Keynotes. Her repeated failure didn't mean that she would not overcome her fears, she just had to remind herself not to give up. After all, tomorrow is another day, and perhaps, the answer is in why the land choose her, when it could have chosen anyone.

Chapter Four
Quest of the Oracle

In the Land of Sozo, the Keynotes were about to learn a special lesson. That no matter how gifted you may be, no one is all knowing. However, if you are willing to seek wisdom, wisdom always leaves clues and somehow finds its way to you.

About this time, in the Treble Clef Kingdom, a bright morning star did appear, high in the sky.

"This is puzzling!" the King said. "It is written, a bright morning star shall appear, a light shining in a dark place, until the day dawns and the morning rises in our hearts!"

Odis, who lived on the first moon in the Outer Spaces, just above the staff, was summoned to the Land of Sozo Council. Although Odis was young, he was the brightest of the oracles.

Odis greeted the King, who immediately began to explain his dilemma with the appearance of the new bright star. Odis sought the future before responding to the King's request. Sadly, he could not explain the prophecy of the star nor the star's future.

"This is most troubling," Odis said.

Pausing, Odis continued, "However, there is one that might have the answers you seek."

Once again, Odis paused and closed his eyes. This time, he sought the future of the Great Oracle.

"We must go on a quest," Odis said as he opened his eyes. "I will need your best Keynotes for the journey."

The King sent for the bravest in the land, as Odis requested.

"I will also need a certain group of special Sozosians."

The King looked a bit puzzled, but agreed to grant Odis request.

"I will need a Pooka, a Shape Shifter, an Edgend of Potion, and Pully the Key Maker," Odis told the King.

The King granted Odis his request, leaving him to gather his team. It wasn't long before Odis assembled his team of five: himself, Michael the Pooka, the fourth space of the Treble Clef; Le' Cat, the third space of the Treble Clef; Billy, the oldest and wisest Edgend; and Pully the Key Maker. These five—the chosen—began their quest with the Keynotes the King had chosen.

Soon they arrived at the Towers of Brave Hearts. There, before them, was a door enthroned in a mountain, shaped like the giant head of a beast. No'

Moda, seeing the Keynotes through her mirror, placed her favorite staff, and then a carved four-eyed snake, through the mirror and touched the ground where the Keynotes were standing. The ground began to shake as Odis put his hand on the heart-shaped knocker, and the Keynotes began to shout.

"We're sinking!"

An inscription appeared on the door. It read,

"If it's getting out of sinking sand that you seek,
Then a heart you must keep.
Open doors with a single arrow;
The shot must be true, straight, and narrow."

"What does that mean?" one of the brave Keynotes yelled.

"It is a riddle. It speaks of a true descendent of the Valentine-Revell family, the third space of the Treble Clef," Odis explained. "Le' Cat, can you shoot one of your arrows into the heart on the door?"

Le' Cat reached into his quiver, retrieved his arrow, and carefully aimed his bow at the doorknocker. With a harmonious zing, the arrow met its mark—the center of the door's heart. Instantly, the sinking sand lifted the Keynotes as the ground became solid once more. No' Moda was furious and even more curious as to who sent the riddle.

The Keynotes sighed with relief as they walked through to what appeared to be an endless hallway of yet, more doors. The Keynotes tried, unsuccessfully, to open some of the doors.

Rattled, the Keynotes told Odis, "There's no way out!"

In a calm voice, the young Oracle said, "There is always a way out."

"Which door?" Le' Cat responded in a calm voice.

Once again, Odis closed his eyes for a moment to consult the Oracle's future. Opening his eyes, he said, "Someone has left us a clue, look for a door with a riddle."

As Michael walked the halls, he found an oversized hand carved door that seemed out of place. On the top of the door was a riddle, just as Odis had predicted.

"Found it!" Michael called out.

He began to read the riddle aloud:

"Think you are a Keynote of means or that you hold the key?
Then knock two times, and you will see.
To open the door, give it a shout.
Either you open this door, or you don't get out.
Find the right words that make up the key.
Here is a clue; you'll need more than you see."

Everyone turned to the wise old Key Maker who laughed and said, "I just happen to have such a key."

He pulled out a key in the shape of the word "shout" and handed it to Odis. Odis placed the key inside the keyhole of the door, knocked two times, and then turned the key, opening the door.

Everyone held their breath as they looked into the room. Inside, the room was covered with mirrors set up like a maze.

No' Moda, once again reached her staff through the mirror. This time she touched the mirrors, and the maze began to change before them.

"Quickly," Odis said. "Maybe there's another clue."

Suddenly, another riddle appeared on the door.

"This is a circle, but it's not one of fun.
See yourself in the mirror; you're sure to be done.
Looking for the door, you'll find it a chore.
Surrounded by mirrors, it's located on the floor."

"Michael, do you think that you can handle that?" Odis asked.

"Already on it," he said.

Michael concealed himself, and then ran through the maze several times before he found the center.

At the center of the maze, on the floor, was another door, just as the riddle has predicted. Once Michael opened the door, the mirrors recessed into the floor.

They all entered the room, and then jumped through the door landing in a beautiful garden. One by one, each fell to the ground. Looking up, they saw a giant tree with a sign that read:

"If a path is what you seek
Then going back will be a treat.

They walked a little further, and then attached to another tree was a sign that read:

*"You have to know that your path ends here.
If you find what you seek, it will disappear."*

Odis asked Billy to talk to some of the Elephant Trees and see if they could lead them to the Great Oracle. One of the trees, who was called Chesup, revealed a passageway through his trunk. When they walked through, they could see the Great Oracle in a small tree house nearby.

"Great!" Odis shouted.

Once they arrived at the tree house, Odis paid his respects to the Great Oracle and said, "Wise and Great Oracle, Elvis, our King, has sent us on a quest to find you."

The Great Oracle replied, "No' Moda, a bright and morning star, time is close. Even as we speak, her power and domain is growing. Tell the King, the hope he seeks is also found in the weakness of the morning star through the human child. Through her, No' Moda will cause destruction, and through her, No' Moda will be defeated."

Before Odis could ask another question, he found himself back in the King's castle along with everyone who was with him on the quest.

When the King saw the Keynotes, he pointed to a room, "Quickly…come inside."

Entering the room, they saw ten other Keynotes talking among themselves. The King said, "I'm glad that I caught you before you went on your quest. I have gathered some of the greatest thinkers in the Land of Sozo. These are our Time Signatures and well… they know everything there is to know about signs in the land."

As the Sozosians continued talking, they became louder and louder.

"What just happened?" Le' Cat asked.

"What do you mean?" the King said as he waved his hands for everyone to quiet down.

"We were just with the Great Oracle."

Le' Cat detailed the message from the Oracle to the King. The King had a puzzled look on his face.

"How… you never left the courtyard."

Odis paused, and then he said, "You have to know that your path ends here. If you find what you seek, it will disappear…the riddles were clues sent from the Great Oracle…we never went to find him. Instead, in his wisdom, the Great Oracle came and found us. Now I understand… ask and it shall be given, seek and you will find, knock and the doors will open."

Chapter Five
No'Moda

In the unseen realm, No'Moda heard voices carried through the wind, speaking of Alley and the *Spaces of the Treble Clef* book. No'Moda devised her own plan; after all, she had one mirror left. This mirror accessed the Land of Sozo; but through this mirror, she would find a way back into the human world.

No'Moda used the mirror to pin herself into the book. When Alley opened the *Spaces of the Treble Clef* to read, a new chapter appeared as No'Moda. She pinned herself as a princess, trapped in a palace until someone strong and brave could rescuer her. No'Moda, with her blue dress and pale skin, stood beside her loyal companion, a white lion named Atrayal. When Alley turned the page of the book, her eyes were enchanted by No'Moda's beauty.

Unbeknown to Alley, No'Moda needed blood with life in it, to give life to her mirrors. On the next page of the book, No'Moda offered Alley a single blue rose. When Alley accept it, she pricked her finger on one of the thorns. With that prick, a single drop of blood was cast down through the mirror, setting into motion a chain of events that no one in the Land of Sozo was prepared for.

Chapter Six
Le' Cat and the Twelve Spies

Alley turned to the next chapter, entitled *Le' Cat and the Twelve Spies*. Alley smiled, remembering him from the palace. He was quite the charmer, she thought. She settled in and quickly became immersed in the pages of the book, once again.

The Keynotes were about to face fear, and at times their fear would only be surpassed by their perception of the task in front of them

Upon the news of No' Moda's return, King Elvis wanted to send spies into the Unseen Realm. The King plotted to send twelve Keynotes to spy on No' Moda. When Le 'Cat told the King he knew of a secret entrance, the King was pleased and gave Le' Cat his blessing. He told the twelve to accompany Le' Cat on his journey.

"But first, this needs a ladies touch," he said in his usual flitting manner.

Off he went to find Allace and Dee Flutter; both Merfish possess rare gifts. Allace has the ability to control water, while Dee Flutter has the ability to retrieve thoughts from the mind.

Walking and talking in the Garden of Escape, the girls heard an odd noise. They spun around to see who—or what—was following them.

Surprised to see a shadowy figure in the brush, Allace called out, "Who's there?"

"It's me," Le' Cat said while stepping out from the shadows.

"Who?" Allace asked, looking at her sister laughing.

Le' Cat confidently walked up and formally introduced himself.

"I am Nigel Miguel Valentine-Revell, but you can call me Le' Cat. At your service," he said with an exaggerated bow.

They giggled at his formal introduction and offered him a curtsy in return.

"Where might you be going on this fine morning?" Le' Cat asked with a grin.

"On a stroll," Dee Flutter replied.

Le' Cat paused for a moment, and then continued, "My family represents the third space of the Treble Clef Staff. Perhaps you have heard of me?" Le' Cat said with pride.

"I don't think so," Allace said. "What do you do?"

Offended, Le' Cat snapped his fingers, and changed his attire.

"I'm a shape shifter," he said with a smile. The Merfish began to laugh and clap with joy.

"Oh . . . . . .oh . . . . . .turn into something great, —like a phoenix," Dee Flutter said with excitement.

Le' Cat bowed his head in shame and said, "I haven't quite mastered that yet. The only thing I've mastered is changing my clothes and locations."

"Well, what good is that?" Dee Flutter said sharply.

De Flutter had no more gotten the words out of her mouth before Le' Cat snapped his fingers again. This time he was wearing a green hooded robe.

"What are those for?" Allace asked.

"Well," Le' Cat said with a smile, "The King has asked me to save the kingdom from No' Moda."

"No' Moda!" The girls gasped.

"I thought you might want to help!" He said with excitement.

The girls smiled. "So you need us?"

"You might say that," Le' Cat answered. The girls looked at each other and then agreed.

"We do love a good intrigue," Allace replied formally, poking fun at Le' Cat. "So where are we going?"

"Our trip takes us to a secret passage under the seas," Le' Cat replied.

Le' Cat snapped his fingers and transported everyone to the entrance. Once at the entrance, they saw a beautiful glass piano. The walls separating the ocean were like skyscrapers, encasing a set of double doors.

"Allace …," Before Le' Cat could finish, Allace waved her hands and parted the waters of the ocean until there was a path of dry land on the ocean's floor. Le' Cat bowed to thank Allace, and she blushed in return.

Le' Cat sat down at the piano and began to play. As he played the "sea" scale—cat, dog, elephant, fish, giraffe, ape, bear, cat—the doors opened.

As they entered through the double doors the water became like glass, and they could see even the lowest level of the seas. They were absolutely mesmerized by how beautiful everything was.

"Ladies, please stay here for a moment, and let us go ahead to confirm your safety," Le' Cat told the girls.

"You know how to contact us if you should need us," Allace said to Le' Cat.

He smiled to confirm he understood.

The Merfish agreed, and the five chosen took the lead while the twelve Keynotes followed at some distance.

When they came to the borders of the Unseen Realm, there stood a single mirror suspended in mid-air. It was unlike anything they had imagined. It was plush, beautiful, and all the colors were more vibrant somehow. No' Moda didn't seem to be suffering at all; indeed, it was quite the opposite.

Once they entered through the mirror, they could see her castle off in the distance and began their journey, trying to stay out of sight.

The locals, known as Seerers of the land, paid them no attention. However, the twelve Keynotes saw the Seerers as a threat.

"We will perish among these giants," they said.

Le' Cat tried to calm them down, and then sent them back to the border.

"Wait for us there," Le' Cat demanded.

Le' Cat, now left with the five chosen, went to the castle. But before entering, he checked to make sure Dee Flutter could read his thoughts.

"Dee Flutter, can you hear me..." Le' Cat said.

"Yes," Dee Flutter responded.

"Great!" Le' Cat replied.

"No' Moda might already know we're here. Be on the look out!" Le' Cat cautioned.

Once inside the castle, they split up. Le' Cat quickly found No' Moda's mirrors in the west wing of her palace. The room looked as if it were stuck in time, surrounded by broken mirrors and a dusty oversized chandelier.

This room must have been a grand ballroom once, but now it was the only part of No' Moda's palace that wasn't maintained. A reminder to No' Moda of the day Levi the Great destroyed her mirrors.

Le' Cat walked over and touched one of the mirrors. Dee Flutter and Le' Cat instantly heard No' Moda giving instruction to Atrayl, her loyal servant and the King with whom she shared her throne.

"Create a single blue rose; it must be beautiful and irresistible. We will offer this rose to Alley and when she accepts, I will have the blood I need to create a mirror into the human world." No' Moda said.

Once Alley read her name on the pages of the book, she became confused and threw the book across the room.

"I thought this was the history of the Land of Sozo." Alley said aloud. "How is my name written in the book? How is this possible?"

Alley would walk away from the book for seven days. Those seven days, Alley was plagued by dreams of Michael and the Kingdoms he had shown her in the Land of Sozo, until finally, she gathered enough strength to pick up the book and continue reading the stories.

Once the group knew the truth, they quickly went to leave the Unseen Realm. But they came face to face with Atrayl and a group of Seerers. The five chosen began to battle with No' Moda's Seerers. The battle with Atrayl pushed them further and further until they were fighting directly in front of the mirror, and then something unusual happened.

Atrayl turned to Le' Cat and said, "Leave now and remember, I will always serve the Queen."

Le' Cat wondered why Atrayl let them go.

Once back in the Land of Sozo, Le' Cat returned the girls home to Mayflower Valley.

As the Merfish walked away, Le' Cat reminded them, "My name is Nigel Miguel Valentine-Revell, but you may call me Le' Cat."

Then Le' Cat and the Keynotes went to inform the King of all that had transpired.

There was just one problem. Le' Cat and the five he had chosen saw things differently from the twelve spies. The twelve spies were convinced that destruction was upon them all.

While Le' Cat was planning an attack for the coming days, he was convinced No' Moda's season of destruction was over, and this new season brought death, not to the Land of Sozo, but to No' Moda herself. No' Moda's plan would ultimately fail. She would be destroyed, and they would take over her kingdom!

The King wanted to sleep on the matter. In the morning, the King arose and sent for Le' Cat.

"We are ready for No' Moda," the King said, "But, let's not rush into battle tomorrow, we need time to plan our attack!" Le' Cat nodded.

Alley was happy that the Seerers let Le' Cat and the Keynotes go.

"That was a close one!" Alley admitted.

Even though Le' Cat hadn't quite mastered being a shape shifter, he was creative and accomplish the task the King had given him.

The idea that it was close, but somehow they were still safe, resonated with her. It was time to face what she needed to do. She had to go and teach the preschool class. She gathered her wits, and prepared herself, she wondered what the other kids in her class might think of her. She realized this could be an opportunity like Le' Cat said, or perhaps the spies were right, defeat was around the corner. The choice of what to believe now solely rested with Alley.

Chapter Seven
Michael the Pooka

The next day, while Alley was in her preschool room, she remembered what the teacher had said, "teaching the preschoolers about music was a big part of her grade." Then she spied her favorite book from the stack of books she brought with her. She couldn't resist picking up the book, *The Ape in the Mirror*.

"This will be a good place to start." She thought.

Alley called all the preschoolers over and began to read them the story. By the time Alley had finished reading the special picture book, she was magically transformed into the Chromatic Ape in the mirror.

She took the children over to the mirror in the classroom and began waving her arms at her reflection. She giggled as she spun around while looking at herself. Then, all the children flooded Alley with questions. Alley explained to the children that this is a fun way to learn music.

Alley peered into the mirror, her eyes wide with wonder. She couldn't believe what she was seeing.

There before her—instead of the trail of mirrors that she expected to see—was Michael. As the children begged Alley to teach them more about music, Michael interrupted.

"Hi, I'm Michael," he said.

"Oh!" Alley shouted, jumping back. "You startled me."

"Good morning," the Keynote said.

You're Michael, the red elephant from the fourth space of the Treble Clef Staff, right?" Alley asked. Michael nodded yes.

Just then, Alley had a thought, "everyone say hello to Michael. He's going to help us today!" Alley told the children. "I want everyone to come over to the piano." Alley decided to use Michael to teach the kids about the fourth space of the Treble Clef.

Michael smiled back at Alley and quickly came in through the mirror. Michael allowed Alley and the kids to pick him up.

Then Tina, one of the preschoolers, said, "I've never seen a red elephant. What kind of elephant are you?"

"Well, I'm a Pooka," Michael replied.

"A Pooka? But what is a Pooka?" Tina asked.

Unsure of how to explain, Michael stumbled around his words a little then finally said, "Well, a Pooka is a very special friend."

"I know!" Alley said interrupting his with a plan. "Let's go to the library and look it up."

Alley took the kids, hid Michael in her book bag, and headed for the library. She went straight to the librarian. She asked her if she had ever heard of a Pooka.

"A Pooka…hmm…," the Librarian said, raising her eyebrow at Alley. "I don't think so. Let's look it up."

Alley squirmed anxiously as she waited for the librarian to look through the records. It didn't take long before the librarian turned back to Alley with a smile.

"Well, how about that," the librarian said with a grin. "We actually have several books on Pookas."

The librarian wrote down the index numbers and handed them to Alley. Alley took the preschoolers and began pulling the books from the shelf, excited to find out more about this Pooka. She opened the first book, *The Legend of the Pooka*, and began reading aloud to the kids.

"A Pooka is a nine-foot to eleven-foot creature of Irish folklore. It can appear as an animal and often hides its true identity," Alley read. "It is said that the Pooka hides its true identity and remains invisible unless it chooses to show itself. If it shows itself, it often takes the form of a nine to eleven-foot animal. The legend goes on to say, that every name has true meaning into the soul. If you can gain the Pooka's trust, it will tell you its name, and you will see its true form."

Alley closed the book and began to talk to the kids about what she had just read to them. She picked up one of the other books, Mischievous Mythical Creatures. This book simply said that Pookas were very large, mischievous animals, and they took the form of a nine-foot elephant, rabbit, or ape.

"Okay—I have seen you grow larger but what does it mean by true form?" Alley said aloud. Michael climbed out of Alley's book bag and stood on to the table.

"True form —" the Pooka paused.

"My true form...was a human boy," he said looking shameful. "I was a warrior to the King of the Unseen Realm!"

Alley paused, almost taken back by the Pooka's revelation.

"Unseen Realm," she repeated.

As soon as she said this, the Pooka was surrounded by light, and a small, human boy, around sixteen years old, appeared before her.

"Oh my! You're a kid!" Alley exclaimed.

The young boy hung his head.

"But, how? Why?" Alley asked.

"As punishment," the boy explained. "From No'Moda. I betrayed her and stole a single red rose from her garden that would one day restore the rightful heir. She judged my actions as treason and turned me into a Pooka. I was forced to leave my family, never to return."

Alley and the preschoolers were sad for Michael.

They quickly returned to the classroom so the kids could be dismissed to the next teacher. The kids shared with Michael how much they loved the time they spent with him, and told him they wanted him to come back often.

Once the kids left the classroom, Alley had a moment alone with Michael. Michael told her it had been two-hundred years, and that he knew the day to defeat No'Moda was coming soon.

"I am ready to defeat her and restore the Unseen Realm," he said.

Then Michael handed Alley a single red rose.

"Is this the rose?" Alley ask.

"It is! The daughter of Eve, chosen to restore the kingdom, will have a birthmark shaped like an apple."

Alley pulled her hair to one side and revealed her birthmark.

"You are the one! The King and Middleton have sent me here to give you this, and you know what you must do." Michael told her.

Alley thanked the Pooka as he gave her the instructions to seek the Merfish. Alley couldn't quite explain it, but she was fearful. She wasn't sure why, or what she was afraid of. But, somehow, she was afraid that No'Moda could hear everything that had just transpired, and she was right.

"The King and that Cat has gone too far with their prophecies. I have a prophecy of my own to fulfill." No' Moda said.

She called for her loyal men to keep Alley away from the Merfish, at all cost. "She must not find the map!" She insisted.

Chapter Eight
Tales of the Merfish

No'Moda set out to stop Alley who now possessed a red rose.

"Capture Alley at once! She must never make it to the Spirit Well with the rose," she insisted.

They planned to capture Alley as soon as she came through the mirror to see the Merfish. However, their plan didn't quite go as they had expected. After Alley finish reading the book, The Ape in the Mirror, instead of one, eight Merfish now appeared in the mirror. They waved at Alley and motioned for her to come to the Land of Sozo. Instead, Alley invited them to come inside her room.

"Can you come through the mirror like Michael?" Alley asked.

"Not sure," Allace the Merfish, replied.

"I don't see why not," Lady Fairy insisted.

Alley held out her hand for Lady Fairy as the other Merfish stared, waiting to see what happened. Once they saw Lady Fairy inside, they flooded Alley's bedroom. Alley was excited that there were Merfish everywhere.

"Have you read your story?" Alley asked the Merfish.

When they nodded no, Alley settled into the bed and read aloud what the Spaces of the Treble Clef had to say about their history.

The magical Land of Sozo holds many mysteries yet to be revealed. Today, the Keynotes were about to find an Alien tribe destined to be a space on our music staff. There's just one problem, they believe they were destined for earth. With some convincing, the Merfish was about to learn a valuable lesson, and that lesson is that nothing just happens. There are no accidents, incidence, or small minute details of our lives that are not orchestrated into their ultimate purpose.

"Wait, wait, wait! That's all wrong, and I'm not an Alien," Bluebell said with some attitude. "I'm human or at least I was."

Shocked by the revelation, Alley said, " You're human...I don't understand."

"Perhaps, before you read any more, we have some explaining to do." Bluebell said and Alley agreed.

Bluebell quickly introduced herself and her sisters. "Well, I'm Bluebell, and these are my sisters Dee Flutter, Ivy, Lady Fairy, Almond Blossom, Allace, Zennia, and Penny Royal."

"Our world was taken over by horrible, mean Belks," Allace told her.

"What's a Belk?" Alley interrupted.

"Belks are heartless humans that have been entangled with animals," Allace replied.

Alley gasped at the thought of humans being entangled with animals.

"That's what I...I mean, we are…well, sort of...we're entangled, but we're not Belks," Allace stated firmly.

"Entangled? But, how did you get entangled, and more importantly, how do we get you untangled?" Alley asked.

Then, Allace lowered her eyes. "Getting entangled was a lot easier than being untangled," she confessed.

"When the fighting broke out between No'Moda and the King, my mom put us in portals to send us to the human world in hopes of saving us," Allace continued. "You see, without the King, we were not protected from No'Moda."

"I don't follow," Alley said with some confusion in her voice. "If you were human, how did you become Merfish?"

"You see, death on earth is supposed to be like being born; only this time, you are born in paradise. But, somehow, some humans got entangled with animals because their heart wasn't full of love, and they were sent to the world of Ork.

"Ork? Is that where you are from?" Alley asked.

Allace shook her head yes, and then she continued explaining. "Ork was never intended for humans, but somehow we've been given a second chance." Allace said.

Looking into everyone's faces, Allace continued explaining. "It is the human heart that guides us home. Like a beacon, it takes humans to paradise. When a human moves away from a pure heart of love, that beacon gets dimmer and dimmer, and in the case of the Belks, it completely goes out. But there is a prophecy that says that if we can change one human heart; our hearts will be changed as well. Our beacon will shine bright again, and it will lead us home."

"A prophecy," Alley repeated.

"Yes...there is a map that will lead to the Spirit Well. This water, with the gift of the red rose given by the daughter of Eve, will bring forth life to all mankind. The secret location is a wooded, enchanted forest called Pixel Layer," Allace said.

"There is just one problem!" Ivy said, cutting across Allace. "We don't actually know that it exists."

Alley looked from Allace to Ivy and then back to Allace.

"Is this the map to Pixel Layer," Alley said as she turned to the next page, in the Spaces of the Treble Clef book, which had a map.

The young Merfish's faces lit up with a big smile as they nodded in agreement.

Alley continued reading the story of how the Merfish came to the Land of Sozo and took on the assignment of becoming the first space of the Treble Clef Staff.

The story explained that in the Treble Clef Kingdom, the Treble Clef Staff has five lines and four spaces.

Given the assignment by Billy the goat he explained, "They—well, all of them—will represent the first space of the music staff here in the Land of Sozo."

The story also revealed that the Merfish destiny was directly linked to the Daughter of Eve's promise, and they would need to join forces in order to find the water that would restore life.

Alley looked at the map and said, "I think I know where this is. It's not too far from here."

Alley put the information into her phone's map system, and they all agreed to seek out the water. Once there, they found nothing but woods. The map on Alley's phone had taken her to what was called, Lakeside Park. Once they had arrived at the park, they had to actually follow the map that was in the book.

Neither Alley nor the Merfish were great at reading a map, but they found a few landmarks. It wasn't long before they found a running river.

"We found it!" The Merfish said.

The River had a waterfall running into a river that ran off into a Well that the town's people used to drink from. Alley looked at the water, and although it was exactly what was described, she felt that somehow, this was not the right well. She just couldn't shake the feeling.

She carefully looked at the map again, it seemed to be in the right place, and it was a Well. Then she looked to see if there was any other well on the map. Sure enough, Jacobs well was on the map.

She told the Merfish, "Let's go see what Jacobs well looks like."

When she found Jacob's well, it was nothing like she had imagined. The Well was made of glass, and up near the top, was a waterfall with two Wells on top of each other. They took the shape of an hourglass with the top flowing to the bottom. But no water was flowing; they were empty.

Alley went to take a closer look, and then noticed that beside the well was a glass pail. She lifted the glass pale and the water in the well flowed from the top to the bottom. This water was snow white, and Alley quickly put the rose into the water.

"This is the right well," she said to the Merfish.

Alley put the red rose Michael had given her into the water, and a map and another book lowed out.

Then the water spoke, "I have been waiting for you. Alley, you have been chosen to save the Land of Sozo. It will not be easy, but it is your purpose, and only you save them. In your gift, you will find everything you need to accomplish this task. As you give your gift, it will give you strength, and with every major turn you must make, there will be a book and a map to guide you through that turn. The Merfish are chosen to assist you with whatever you need. Treat them well, and your connection will change the world."

Alley heard her alarm clock ring, and when she awoke, she did not know if the map and the book was just a dream or if it was real. Then she looked on her bedside table. There was both the book that read, Lines of the Treble Clef, and the map to the Unseen Realm.

"Did I restore life?" she thought. What about the Merfish? Where were they? She had answers but those answers seemed to bring more question. Somehow she knew the key to all her answers was in the book she was about to read.

Land of Sozo
Glossary of Terms

Land of Sozo - Where music originates.

Staff - Five lines and four spaces that are the foundation upon which the Keynotes live.

Keynotes - Animals in the Land of Sozo who are assigned to the music staff.

Sozosians - All animals who live in the Land of Sozo.

Musical Alphabet - (C)at-(D)og-(E)lephant-(F)ish-(G)iraffe-(A)pe-(B)ear.

Species - Seven species make up the musical alphabet.

Family Tribal Crest - Each family has its very own family crest, which rests on the flag color that represents the colors on the piano and music staff.

The Ape in the Mirror - Magical book in the human world, which turns human children into Levi the Great, a Chromatic Apes of the second line of the Treble Clef.

Edgend of Potion - The gift to brew potions, create books, with magical properties to influence actions, gestures and language to good.

Kingdoms

Treble Clef Kingdom - The territory of the five lines and five spaces that make up the Treble Clef on the music staff.

Bass Clef Kingdom - The territory of the five lines and five spaces that make up the Bass Clef on the music staff.

Unseen Realm - A breathtaking world inhabited by Seerers.

Tribes

Parkadian Dogs - Founders of the Land of Sozo.

Merfish - Half-humans from the After planet of Ork, Merfish escaped the danger of their world to live in the Land of Sozo.

Chromatic Apes - Warriors, the Chromatic Apes were humans who used magic to destroy No'Moda's control trapping them in Ape form forever. They reside in the Land of Sozo, and represent the second space of the Treble Clef.

Valentine-Revell - Representing their space of the Treble Clef. A family composed of shape-shifters. Valentine comes from this family.

Pooka - Very large, mischievous mythical creatures who are mainly invisible and usually appear to humans in the form of a nine-foot elephant, rabbit, or ape.

Oracles - Oracles live on the first moon of outer space. Oracles are capable of seeing both the future and the past.

Middleton Cats - Represents the territory between the treble clef & bass clef.

Main Characters

Tetris
  Species: Dog
  Gift: Sees notes in color
  Assignment: Middle Dee
  Tribe: Parkadians

Levi
  Species: Giraffe
  Gift: Ability to see the future and past
  Assignment: First moon from the Land of Sozo
  Tribe: Oracles

Nigel Miguel Valentine-Revell (Le'Cat)
  Species: Cat
  Gift: Shape-shifter
  Assignment: Third space of the Treble Clef
  Tribe: Valentine-Revell

Michael
  Species: Elephant
  Gift: Invisible
  Assignment: Fourth space of the Treble Clef
  Tribe: Pookas

Alley
   Species: Ape
   Gift: Singing and teaching
   Assignments: Second Space of the Treble Clef
   Tribe: Chromatic Apes

Dee Flutter
   Species: Fish
   Gift: Ability to reading the mind
   Assignment: First Space of the Treble Clef
   Tribe: Merfish

Lady Fairy
   Species: Fish
   Gift: Controls Laughter and Joy
   Assignment: First Space of the Treble Clef
   Tribe: Merfish

Almond Blossom
   Species: Fish
   Gift: Controls the Seasons
   Assignment: First Space of the Treble Clef
   Tribe: Merfish

Blue Bell
   Species: Fish
   Gift: Controls the weather
   Assignment: First Space of the Treble Clef
   Tribe: Merfish

Zennia
   Species: Fish
   Gift: Controls fire
   Assignment: First Space of the Treble Clef
   Tribe: Merfish

Penny Royal
   Species: Fish
   Gift: Princess of Gifts
   Assignment: First space of the Treble Clef
   Tribe: Merfish

Ivy
   Species: Fish
   Gift: Power to control nature
   Assignment: First space of the Treble Clef
   Tribe: Merfish

Allace
   Species: Fish
   Gift: Manipulates water
   Assignment: First space of the Treble Clef
   Tribe: Merfish

Characters

Billy the Goat - Goats were originally chosen to work on the second line of the staff until the giraffe changed the course of Sozo.

Belks - A nickname for those who are heartless and selfish on the planet Ork.

King Middleton - Leader of Middleton

Middleton Cats - Represents Middle C. Their job is to unite the Treble Clef and the Bass Clef Kingdoms.

Elvis - King of Sozo and fourth line of the Treble Clef.

Pully - Key Maker

Land of Sozo Council - A council of Keynotes, which makes decisions for the Land of Sozo.

Great Oracle - The greatest, oldest, and wisest Oracle on the planet Exodus.

No'Moda - Self-appointed ruler of the unseen realm.

Levi the Great - Great human leader transformed himself and his tribe into Ape so that they could slip into the unseen realm and destroy No'Moda's mirrors.

Locations

Babbling Brook - magical brook that can only repeat what it hears.

Ork - Distant planet where animals go after they depart from the human world.

Pixel Layer - Secret Earth location revealed in a prophecy to the Merfish.

Sugar Land Providence - Largest providence in the Treble Clef Kingdom.

Sozo World - The most magical place in the Land of Sozo, a theme park inspired by the Keynotes.

Towers of Brave Hearts - Located on the borders of the Treble Clef Kingdom, this tower examines the true identity of a person.

Land of Sozo
Outer Spaces

Exodus - First moon from the Land of Sozo

Falcore - Second moon from the Land of Sozo

Eritria - Third moon from the Land of Sozo

Lila - Fourth moon from the Land of Sozo

Outer Lines

Star - First sun from the Land of Sozo

Elipsia - Second sun from the Land of Sozo

Hakkas - Third sun from the Land of Sozo

Weidenaars - Fourth sun from the Land of Sozo

Elul - Fifth sun from the Land of Sozo

The Spaces of the Treble Clef *offers an imaginative collection of short stories that represent each letter in the musical alphabet with whimsical animals called Keynotes – cat, dog, elephant, fish, giraffe, ape and bear.*

The Keynotes biblical backstories share a common musical destiny: To teach music to every child on earth. Each story, at its simplest level, is designed to help students identify a piano note, and keys locations on the music staff. This book is part of our 5-part Sozo Music Teaching System that includes the Sozo Keys Piano Book, Pop Academy of Music Storybook, Piano Stickers, Read and Play CD, and Piano Practice Files.

www.ingramcontent.com/pod-product-compliance
Lightning Source LLC
Chambersburg PA
CBHW060518300426
44112CB00017B/2728